# My First
# Cantonese Words

This is an illustrated book to teach basic Cantonese vocabulary.
Each item contains the meaning in Chinese characters, Jyutping and English.
It is suitable for young children as well as whoever is interested to learn beginner Cantonese.

The tables below are to help pronounce 'jyutping' – Cantonese pronounciation.
"Consonants + Vowels + 6-tones pitch" to form a word.

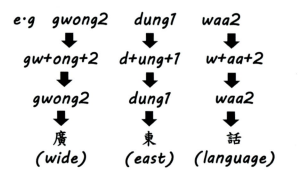

In this case, these 3 single Chinese characters join together form the meaning in English is: **Cantonese**

### Pronunciation Guide

| Consonants | |
|---|---|
| Symbols | Sound in English |
| b | spy |
| c (ts) | bits |
| d | stay |
| f | for |
| g | sky |
| gw | squad |
| h | hall |
| k | kit |
| kw | quiet |
| l | lime |
| m | my |
| n | no |
| ng | hang |
| p | pan |
| s | see |
| t | tan |
| w | west |
| j (y) | yes |
| z | jar |

| Vowels | |
|---|---|
| Symbols | Sound in English |
| i | see |
| yu | union |
| u | mood |
| e | cherry |
| oe | her |
| o | law |
| aa | father |
| **With nasals** | |
| im | seem |
| in | seen |
| ing | sing |
| yun | uno (in spanish) |
| un | soon |
| ung | own + ng (use the sound) |
| eng | length |
| eon | london |
| oeng | earn |
| on | lawn |
| ong | long |
| am | sum |
| an | sun |
| ang | rung |
| aam | arm |
| aan | aunt |
| aang | under |
| m | mm |
| ng | hang |
| **Diphthong** | |
| ui | ruin |
| ei | day |
| eoi | on + boy (similar sound) |
| oi | boy |
| ai | fight |
| aai | aisle |
| iu | few |
| ou | go |
| au | out |
| aau | now |

| Vowels (no sound at the end) | |
|---|---|
| Symbols | Sound in English |
| ip | deep |
| it | eat |
| ik | egg |
| yut | shut |
| ut | foot |
| uk | cook |
| ek | check |
| eot | but |
| oek | lurk |
| ot | sort |
| ok | lock |
| at | butter |
| ap | up |
| aap | sharp |
| aat | art |
| aak | mark |
| ak | yuck |

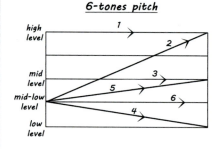

# My First Cantonese Words

Text & Illustrated by Dawn Kwok
Edited by David Walters

First published in Edinburgh 2019
Copyright © 2019 Dawn Kwok
All rights reserved. No part of this book may be reproduced,
without the prior written permission of the copyright owner.

季節
# gwai3 zit3
## Seasons

三月
saam1 jyut6
**march**

四月
sei3 jyut6
**april**

五月
ng5 jyut6
**may**

九月
gau2 jyut6
**september**

十月
sap6 jyut6
**october**

十一月
sap6 jat1 jyut6
**november**

春天
ceon1 tin1
**spring**

秋天
cau1 tin1
**autumn**

# 月份
# jyut6 fan6
# Months

夏天
haa6 tin1
**summer**

六月
luk6 jyut6
**june**

七月
cat1 jyut6
**july**

八月
baat3 jyut6
**august**

冬天
dung1 tin1
**winter**

十二月
sap6 ji6 jyut6
**december**

一月
jat1 jyut6
**january**

二月
ji6 jyut6
**february**

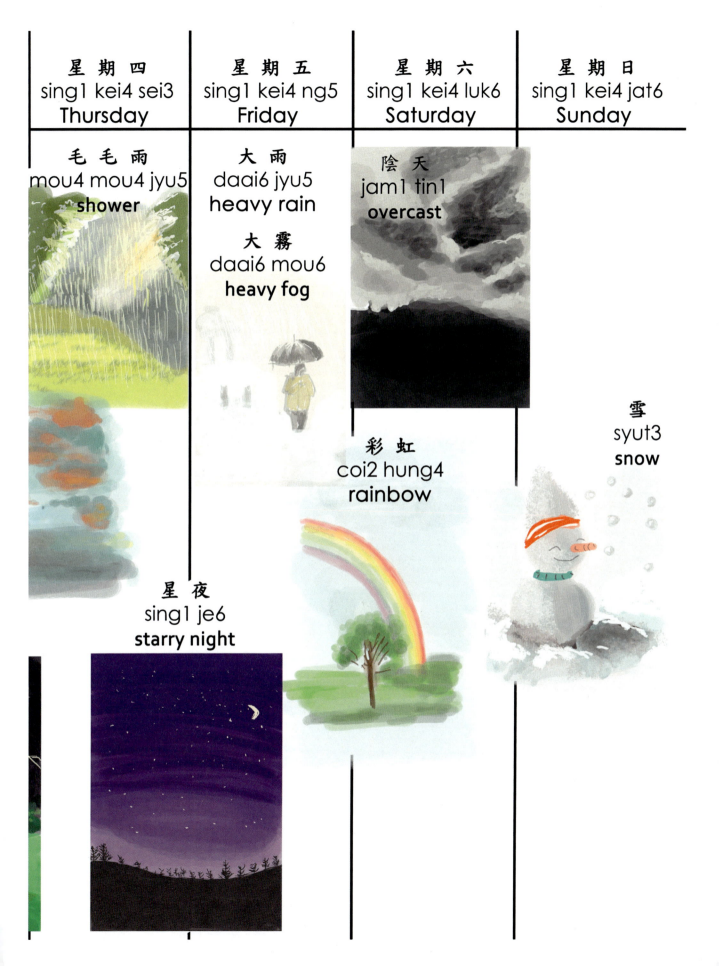

冬天衫
dung1 tin1 saam1
Winter clothes

短褲
dyun2 fu3
shorts

太陽帽
taai3 joeng4 mou6
sun hat

下雨天
haa6 jyu5 tin1
Rainy day

穿什麼?
**cyun1 sam6 mo1**
**What to wear?**

涼鞋
loeng4 haai4
sandals

夏天衫
haa6 tin1 saam1
Summer clothes

水鞋
seoi2 haai4
wellington boots

# 顏色
## ngaan4 sik1
## Colour

紅色
hung4 sik1
red

橙色
caang4 sik1
orange

黃色
wong4 sik1
yellow

淺綠色
cin2 luk6 sik1
light green

深綠色
sam1 luk6 sik1
**dark green**

粉紅色
fan2 hung4 sik1
**pink**

淺藍色
cin2 laam4 sik1
**light blue**

灰色
fui1 sik1
**grey**

深藍色
sam1 laam4 sik1
**dark blue**

黑色
hak1 sik1
**black**

紫色
zi2 sik1
**purple**

白色
baak6 sik1
**white**

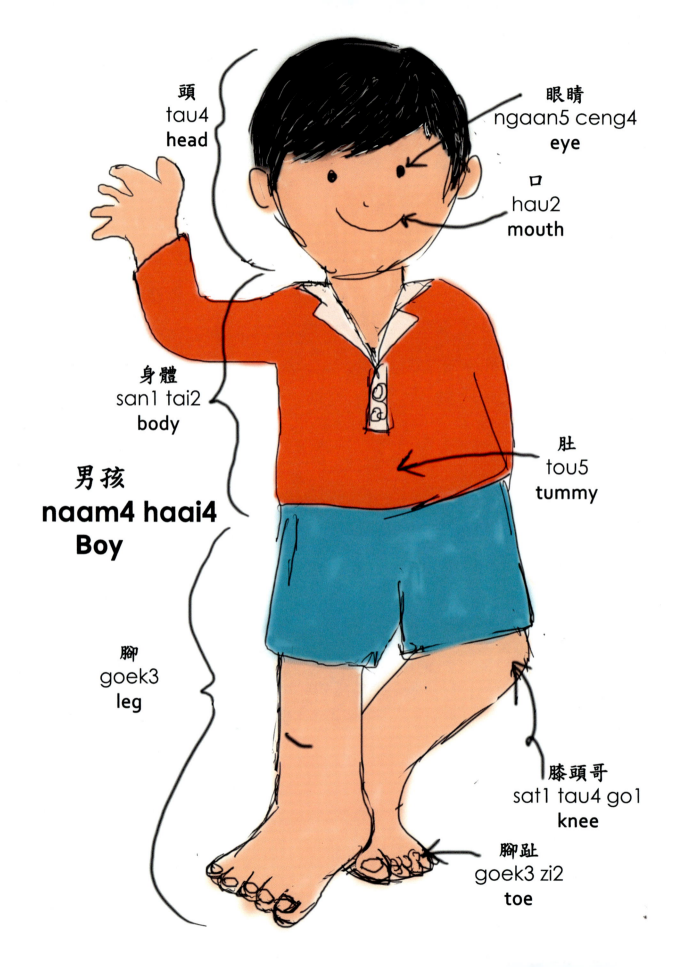

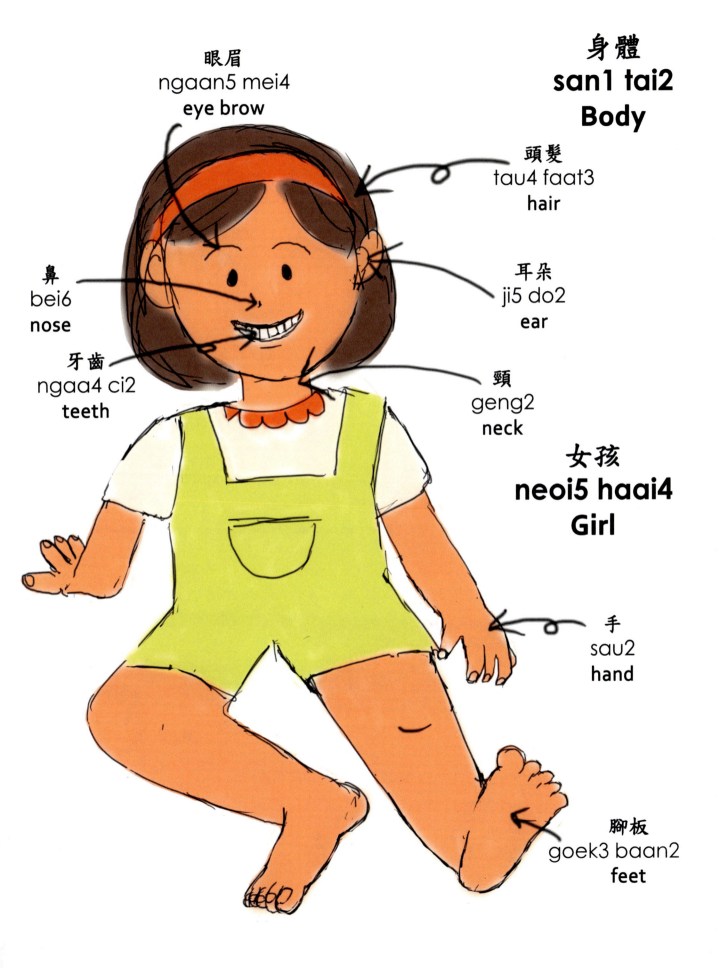

祖父
zou2 fu6
Dad's dad

叔父
suk1 fu6
Dad's brother

嬸嬸
sam2 sam2
Dad's brother's wife

爸爸
baa1 baa1
My dad

堂兄弟姊妹
tong4 hing1 dai6 zi2 mui6
Dad's brother's son/ daughter

姐姐
ze2 ze2
My elder sister

我
ngo5
Myself

---

外祖父
ngoi6 zou2 fu6
Mum's dad

舅父
kau5 fu6
Mum's brother

舅母
kau5 mou5
Mum's brother's wife

姨母
ji4 mou5
Mum's older/ younger sister

 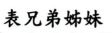
表兄弟姊妹
biu2 hing1 dai6 zi2 mui6
Mum's brother & sister's son/ daughter

# 父系家庭樹
## fu6 hai6 gaa1 ting4 syu6
## Dad's side family tree

祖母
zou2 mou5
Dad's mum

媽媽
maa1 maa1
My mum

姑丈
gu1 zoeng6
Dad's sister's husband

姑媽
gu1 maa1
Dad's older sister

姑姐
gu1 ze2
Dad's younger sister

妹妹
mui6 mui6
My younger sister

弟弟
dai6 dai6
My younger brother

表兄弟姊妹
biu2 hing1 dai6 zi2 mui6
Dad's sister's son/ daughter

---

# 母系家庭樹
## mou5 hai6 gaa1ting4 syu6
## Mum's side family tree

外祖母
ngoi6 zou2 mou5
Mum's mum

姨丈
ji4 zoeng6
Mum's older/ younger sister's husband

爸爸
baa1 baa1
My dad

媽媽
maa1 maa1
My mum

我和我的姊弟妹
ngo5 wo4 ngo5 dik1 zi2 dai6 mui6
Me and my sisters & brother

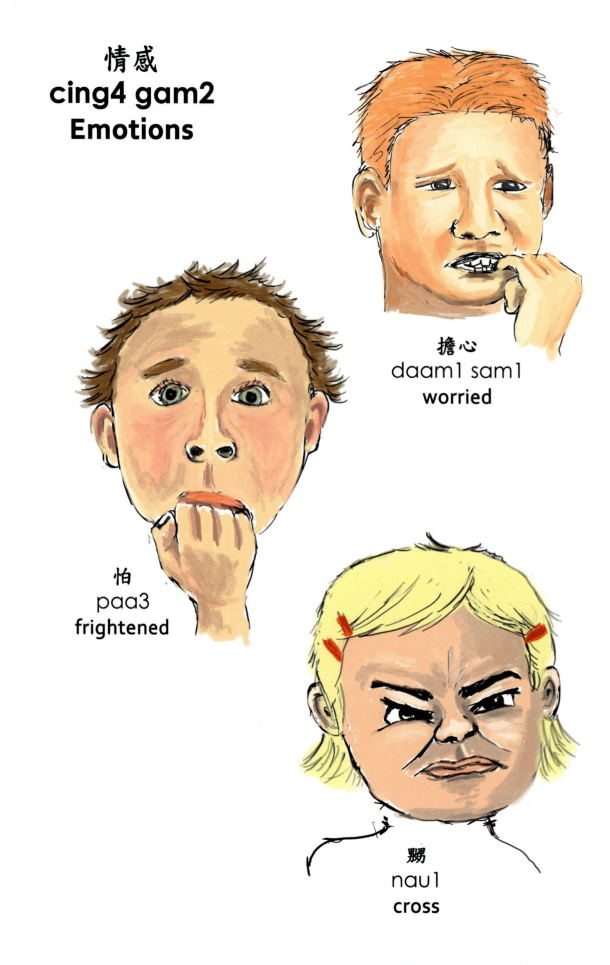

**頑皮**
waan4 pei4
**naughty/ cheeky**

驚訝
geng1 ngaa6
**surprised**

開心
hoi1 sam1
**happy**

傷心
soeng1 sam1
**sad**

哭
huk1
**cry**

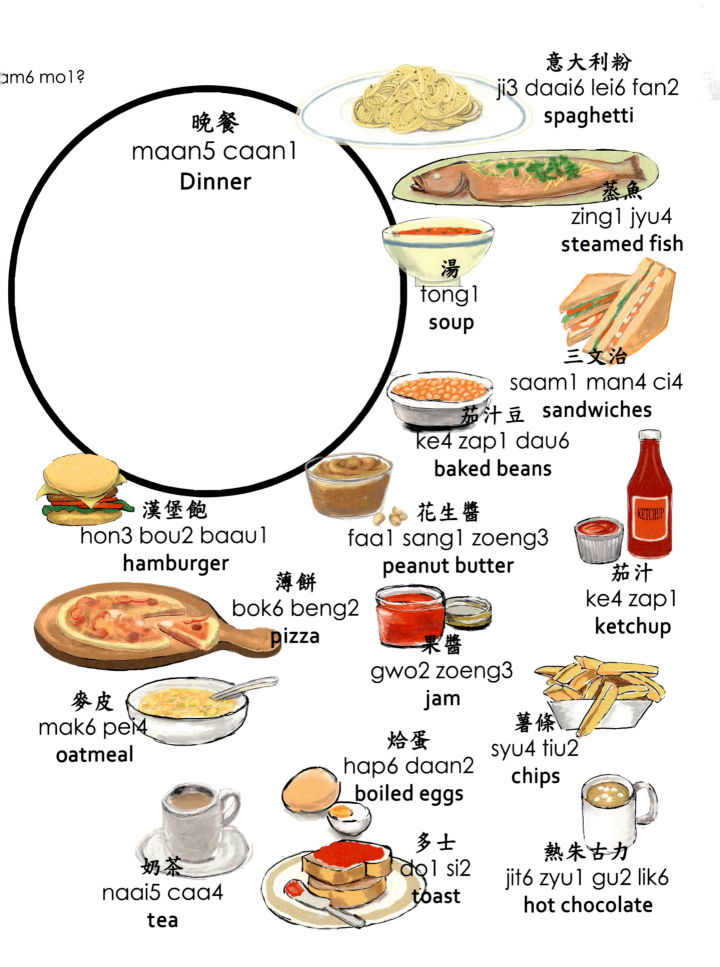

# 餐具
## caan1 geoi6
### Cutlery

筷子
faai3 zi2
chopsticks

刀
dou1
knives

匙羹
ci4 gang1
spoons

叉
caa1
fork

你會用什麼餐具?
nei5 wui5 jung6 sam6 mo1 caan1 geoi6?
What cutlery would you use?

# 甜品
## tim4 ban2
### Dessert

冬甩/甜圈
dung1 lat1/
tim1 hyun1
doughnuts

蛋糕
daan6 gou1
cake

雪糕
syut3 gou1
ice-cream

# 量詞
## loeng6 ci4
### Words of Measurement

兩條薯條
loeng5 tiu4 syu4 tiu2
two chips

一杯茶
jat1 bui1 caa4
a cup of tea

一碗飯
jat1 wun2 faan6
a bowl of rice

兩塊麵包
loeng5 faai3 min6 baau1
two slices of bread

一碟麵
jat1 dip6 min6
a plate of noodles

一隻蛋
jat1 zek3 daan2
an egg

一對筷子
jat1 deoi3 faai3 zi2
a pair of chopsticks

一樽茄汁
jat1 zeon1 ke4 zap1
a bottle of Ketchup

馬卡龍
maa5 kaa1 lung4
macaron

刨冰
paau4 bing1
ice

曲奇餅
kuk1 kei4 beng2
cookie

湯圓
tong1 jyun2
glutinous rice balls

雜誌
zaap6 zi3
**magazines**

茶几
caa4 gei1
**coffee table**

搖控器
jiu4 hung3 hei3
**remote control**

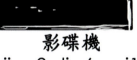

手機
sau2 gei1
**mobile**

影碟機
jing2 dip6 gei1
**DVD player**

相架
soeng3 gaa2
**picture frame**

座地燈
zo6 dei6 deng1
**floor lamp**

地毡
dei6 zin1
**rug**

電視
din6 si6
**television**

# 浴室
# juk6 sat1
# Bathroom

廁紙 ci3 zi2 — toilet roll

梳 so1 — comb

浴帽 juk6 mou2 — shower cap

毛巾 mou4 gan1 — towel

肥皂/番梘 fei4 zou6/ faan1 gaan2 — soap

花灑 faa1 saa1 — shower

浴缸 juk6 gong1 — bathtub

水龍頭 seoi2 lung4 tau4 — tap

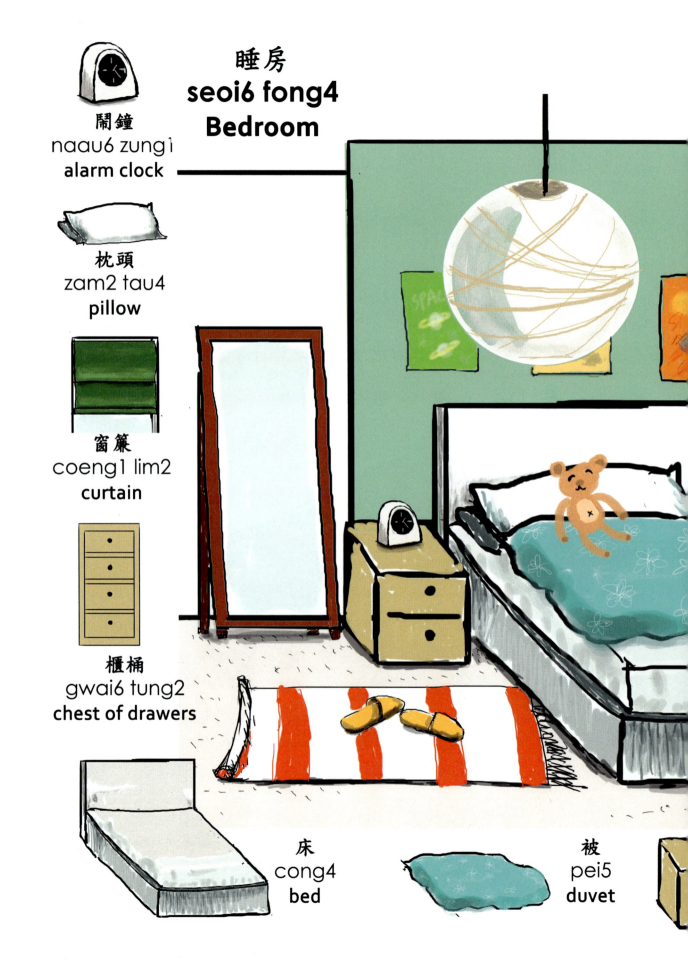

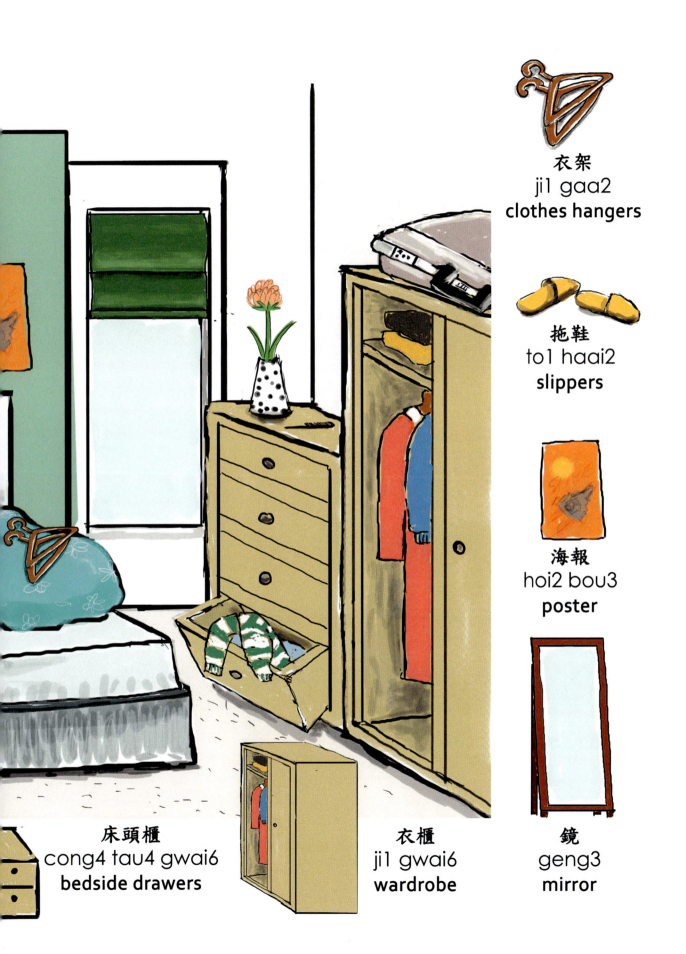

# 課室
## fo3 sat1
## Classroom

投影機
tau4 jing2 gei1
projector

相機
soeng2 gei1
camera

蠟筆
laap6 bat1
crayons

間尺
gaan3 cek3
ruler

顏色筆 / 畫筆
ngaan4 sik1 bat1 /
waa2 bat1
colour pencils /
paint brushes

老師
lou5 si1
teacher

學生
hok6 saang1
pupil

膠水
gaau1 seoi2
**glue**

擦膠
caat3 gaau1
**eraser**

鉸剪/ 剪刀
gaau3 zin2/
zin2 dou1
**scissors**

書
syu1
**books**

魚缸
jyu4 gong1
**fish tank**

電腦
din6 nou5
**computer**

砌圖
cai3 tou4
**puzzle**

# 睇醫生
## tai2 ji1 sang1
## To see the doctor

填顏色
tin4 ngaan4 sik1
Can you colour them up?

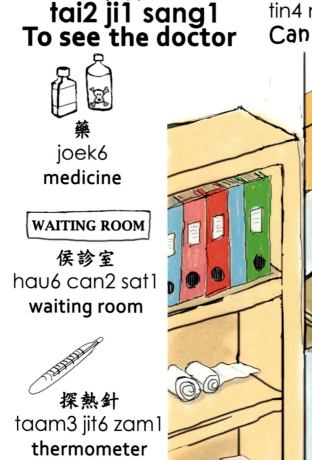

藥
joek6
medicine

侯診室
hau6 can2 sat1
waiting room

探熱針
taam3 jit6 zam1
thermometer

電話
din6 waa2
telephone

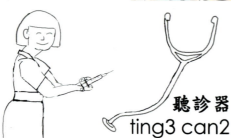

護士
wu6 si6
nurse

聽診器
ting3 can2 hei3
stethoscope

膠布
gaau1 bou3
plaster

拐杖
gwaai2 zoeng2
crutch

醫生
ji1 sang1
doctor

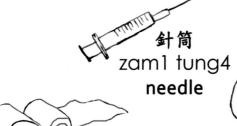
針筒
zam1 tung4
needle

繃帶
bang1 daa3
bandage

血壓計
hyut3 aat3 gai3
blood pressure monitor

病人
bing6 jan4
patient

輪椅
leon4 ji2
wheelchair

沙池
saa1 ci4
sandpit

公園
# gung1 jyun2
**Park**

搖搖板
jiu4 jiu4 baan2
**see-saw**

滑梯
waat6 tai1
**slide**

板凳
baan2 dang3
**bench**

野餐
je5 caan1
**picnic**

攀爬網
paan1 paa4 mong5
**climbing frame**

池塘
ci4 tong4
**pond**

鞦韆
cin1 cau1
swing

跳繩
tiu3 sing2
skipping rope

滑板
waat6 baan2
skateboard

風箏／紙鷂
fung1 zang1/
zi2 jiu2
kite

踏單車
daap6 daan1 ce1
ride a bike

踢波／球
tek3 bo1/ kau4
kick a ball

滾軸溜冰鞋
gwan2 zuk6 lau4 bing1 haai4
roller skates

找找看
zaau2 zaau2 hon3
Can you find them?

城鎮
seng4 zan3
Town

消防車
siu1 fong4 ce1
fire engine

警車
ging2 ce1
police car

雪糕車
syut3 gou1 ce1
ice cream van

噴水池
pan3 seoi2 ci4
fountain

貓
maau1
cat

海鷗
hoi2 au1
seagull

直昇機
zik6 sing1 gei1
helicopter

消防局
siu1 fong4 guk6
fire station

屋
uk1
house

醫院
ji1 jyun2
hospital

教堂
gaau3 tong4
church

酒店
zau2 dim3
hotel

學校
hok6 haau6
school

戲院
hei3 jyun2
cinema

工廠
gung1 cong2
factory

商場
soeng1 coeng4
shopping mall

警局
ging2 guk2
police station

公寓
gung1 jyu6
apartment

郵局
jau4 guk2
post office

超級市場
ciu1 kap1 ci5 coeng4
supermarket

博物館
bok3 mat6 gun2
museum

摩天大廈
mo1 tin1 daai6 haa6
skyscraper

廣場
gwong2 coeng4
square

# 火車站 和 碼頭
## fo2 ce1 zaam6 wo4 maa5 tou4
## Train station & Pier

行李
hang4 lei5
**luggage**

乘客
sing4 haak3
**passenger**

手錶
sau2 biu1
**watch**

自動販賣機
zi6 dung6 faan3 maai6 gei1
**vending machine**

高山
gou1 saan1
**mountain**

船
syun4
boat

車票
ce1 piu3
train ticket

熱氣球
jit6 hei3 kau4
hot air balloon

路軌
lou6 gwai2
train track

街燈
gaai1 dang1
street lamp

月台
jyut6 toi4
platform

# 海洋生物
# hoi2 joeng4 saang1 mat6
# Sea Animals

青口
ceng1 hau2
**mussels**

水母
seoi2 mou5
**jellyfish**

海馬
hoi2 maa5
**seahorse**

魚
jyu4
**fish**

龍蝦
lung4 haa1
**lobster**

海膽
hoi2 daam2
**sea urchin**

蟹
haai5
**crab**

海龜
hoi2 gwai1
turtle

鯊魚
saa1 jyu4
shark

海星
hoi2 sing1
starfish

珊瑚
saan1 wu4
coral

海豚
hoi2 tyun4
dolphin

雞泡魚
gai1 pou5 jyu4
pufferfish

蝦
haa1
prawn

鯨魚
king4 jyu4
whale

# 相反詞與動物
# soeng1 faan2 ci4 jyu5 dung6 mat6
## Opposites (with animals)

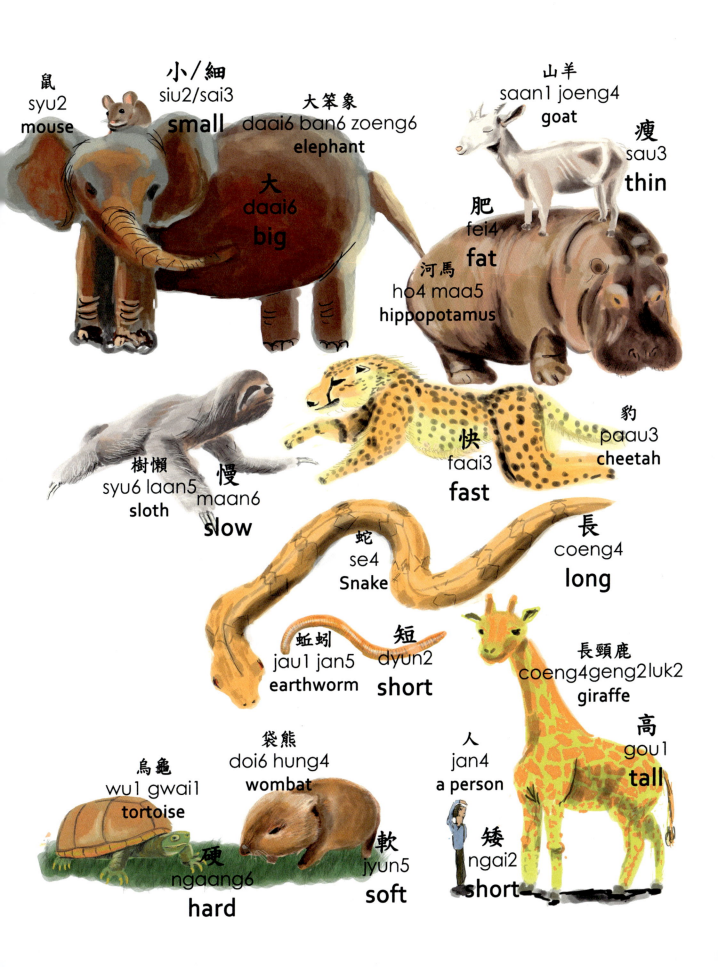

形狀
# jing4 zong6
**Shapes**

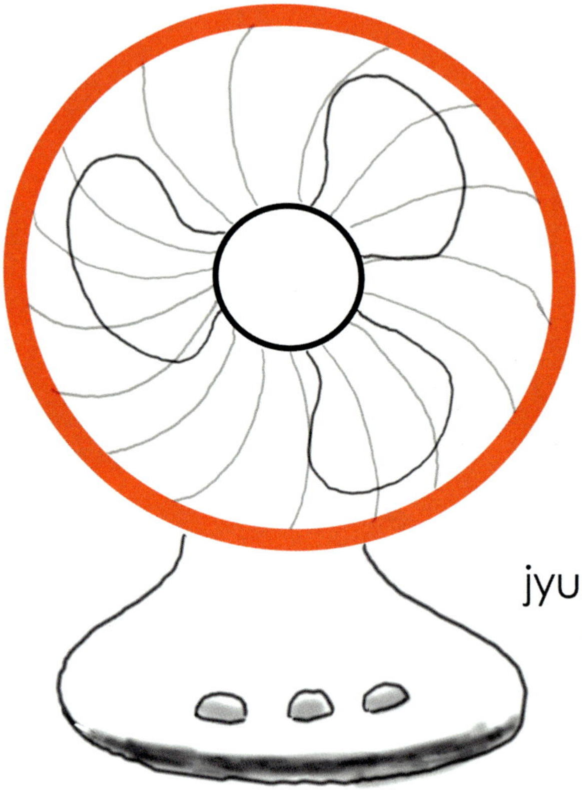

圓形
jyun4 jing4
**circle**

橢圓形
to5 jyun4 jing4
**oval**

星形
sing1 jing4
**star**

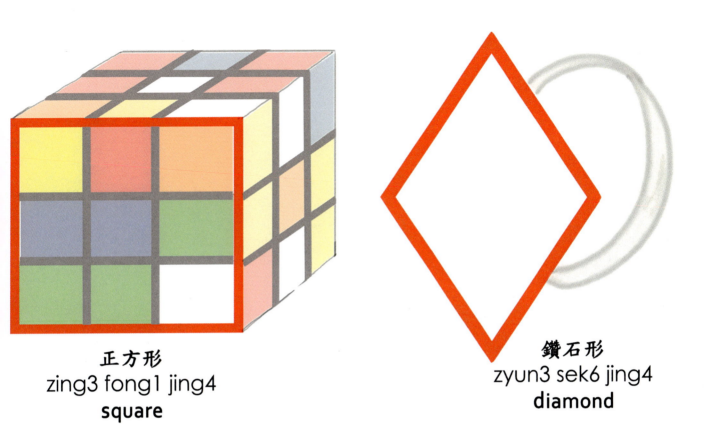

正方形
zing3 fong1 jing4
**square**

鑽石形
zyun3 sek6 jing4
**diamond**

三角形
saam1 gok3 jing4
**triangle**

Made in the USA
San Bernardino, CA
21 May 2020